Building Self-Confidence

by Stuart Schwartz and Craig Conley

Content Consultant:
Robert J. Miller, Ph.D.
Associate Professor
Mankato State University

CAPSTONE BOOKS
an imprint of Capstone Press
Mankato, Minnesota

Capstone Books are published by Capstone Press
151 Good Counsel Drive, P.O. Box 669, Mankato, Minnesota 56002
http://www.capstone-press.com

Copyright © 1998 Capstone Press. All rights reserved.
No part of this book may be reproduced without written permission from the publisher. The publisher takes no responsibility for the use of any of the materials or methods described in this book, nor for the products thereof.
Printed in the United States of America.

Library of Congress Cataloging-in-Publication Data
Schwartz, Stuart, 1945-
   Building self-confidence/by Stuart Schwartz and Craig Conley.
   p.cm. -- (Life skills)
   Includes bibliographical references and index.
   Summary: Explores the development of self-confidence through identifying one's positive qualities and appreciating the qualities of others.
   ISBN 1-56065-720-0
   1. Self-confidence--Juvenile literature. [1. Self-confidence.] I. Conley, Craig, 1965- . II. Title. III. Series: Schwartz, Stuart, 1945- Life skills.
BF575.S39S38 1998
158.1--dc21   97-51298
                                                                             CIP
                                                                              AC

Photo credits:
All photos by Dede Smith Photography

Table of Contents

Chapter 1 Building Self-Confidence 5
Chapter 2 Appearance 7
Chapter 3 Positive Outlook 9
Chapter 4 Taking Action 11
Chapter 5 Feeling Worthwhile 13
Chapter 6 Respecting Differences 15
Chapter 7 Accepting Praise 17
Chapter 8 Accepting Criticism 19
Chapter 9 Taking Steps 21
Chapter 10 Setting Goals 23
Chapter 11 Showing Self-Confidence 25
Chapter 12 Self-Confidence and You 27

Words to Know 28
To Learn More 29
Useful Addresses 30
Internet Sites 31
Index 32

Chapter 1

Building Self-Confidence

People who have self-confidence are often successful. Self-confidence means believing in one's abilities. Self-confident people know they have the skills and abilities to be good workers.

Self-confident people have high self-esteem. Self-esteem is a feeling of pride and respect for oneself. People with high self-esteem believe they are worthwhile. They value themselves.

People can build self-confidence. They can take steps to grow and improve. Learning new skills builds self-confidence. For example, a child care worker can find new ways to care for children. A cook can learn new methods to prepare food.

Building self-confidence is worthwhile. Self-confident people take pride in their work.

Self-confident people have high self-esteem.

Chapter 2

Appearance

Self-confident people feel good about their appearance. They accept the way they look.

People who want to feel self-confident try to look their best. They keep their hair, teeth, and bodies clean. They wear clean clothes.

People can change some parts of their appearance. They can style their hair in new ways. They can exercise to build firmer bodies.

Self-confident people learn to accept what they cannot change. People cannot change other parts of their appearance. For example, they cannot change how short or tall they are.

People can build self-confidence by being proud of their appearance. Self-confident people feel good about how they look.

People can exercise to build firmer bodies.

Chapter 3

Positive Outlook

Most self-confident people have positive outlooks. People with positive outlooks feel confident about the future. They know they can find ways to solve problems. They want to improve.

For example, a mail truck runs out of gas. The driver keeps a positive outlook and does not panic. This helps the driver think clearly. The driver calls a gas station for help. The driver also learns from the mistake. The driver fills the truck with gas more often.

People with positive outlooks know that they cannot control everything that happens. They look for the best answers to problems. For example, a teacher plans to take students to a park. It starts raining. The teacher does not become disappointed. The teacher finds indoor activities for the students. The teacher keeps the students busy until the rain stops.

People with positive outlooks find ways to succeed. Their successes build their self-confidence.

Most self-confident people have positive outlooks.

Chapter 4

Taking Action

People can build self-confidence by taking action. Solving problems is one way to take action. Solving problems helps people feel more confident and successful.

For example, a nurse's car has a flat tire. The nurse reads directions on changing a tire. The nurse puts on a new tire. The nurse has taken action to solve a problem. The nurse feels more confident.

People also can build confidence by helping others. For example, a factory worker may see someone trying to lift a box. The box looks heavy. The worker helps lift the box. The worker has taken action to help someone else.

Helping others makes people feel good about themselves. This builds self-confidence.

People can build confidence by helping others.

Chapter 5

Feeling Worthwhile

Self-confident people feel worthwhile. They have high self-esteem. They value their own opinions.

It is hard for some people to believe in themselves. Instead they may believe what other people say about them. For example, a student is not doing well in a class. The teacher tells the student to work harder. The student may already be working as hard as possible. The teacher's remark may make the student feel discouraged. The student may lose self-confidence.

People can take steps to feel worthwhile. Maybe the student does not understand the subject. The student can ask the teacher for help. This may help the student improve in the subject.

People must work to improve their self-esteem. They need to change the way they think about themselves. Making positive changes helps people believe in themselves.

Self-confident people value their own opinions.

Chapter 6

Respecting Differences

Self-confident people respect themselves. Most self-confident people also respect others.

People can be different in many ways. People may have different opinions and beliefs. They may celebrate different holidays. They may attend different churches.

People who are self-confident can respect the ways that others are different. They understand that they can learn from the opinions and beliefs of others.

For example, two office workers have differing opinions about one part of a project. They set their differences aside. They listen to and respect each other's opinions. They then find the best way to complete this part of the project.

Self-confident people respect others.

Chapter 7

Accepting Praise

Learning to accept praise builds a person's self-confidence. Praise is positive words about a person's actions or appearance. People who are proud of their abilities can accept praise.

Some people find it hard to accept praise. They may have low self-esteem. They may say nothing when someone praises them. They may tell the person that the praise is not true. They may not feel worthy of praise.

Self-confident people know how to accept praise. They thank people for compliments. For example, a baker bakes bread for customers. A customer is a person who buys goods and services. A customer praises the baker's bread. The baker thanks the customer. The baker is proud of working hard to make good bread.

People who are self-confident can accept praise. They feel proud of their work.

Self-confident people know how to accept praise.

Chapter 8

Accepting Criticism

People can build self-confidence by learning to accept criticism. Criticism is pointing out the strengths and weaknesses of others.

Everyone has strengths and weaknesses. For example, a typist may spell poorly. But the typist may also type quickly.

Supervisors may criticize workers for their mistakes. A supervisor is a person who is in charge of workers. A good supervisor offers criticism that helps workers see their strengths and improve their weaknesses. Workers can learn from helpful criticism.

For example, a supervisor may criticize the typist's work. The supervisor points out spelling mistakes. The supervisor teaches the typist to slow down and check work more carefully. The typist slows down and improves spelling. The typist improves by accepting criticism.

Workers can learn from helpful criticism.

Chapter 9

Taking Steps

People can take steps to improve their skills. This will build their self-confidence.

One step people can take is to make a list of their strengths. For example, a cook might list creating new recipes. A flight attendant might list comforting nervous passengers.

People can also list ways they want to improve. For example, an office clerk may want to improve writing skills. A factory worker may want to work more quickly.

Another step people can take is to try new skills. Learning new skills helps build self-confidence.

For example, a student may want to feel more comfortable talking in front of others. The student might decide to try answering more questions. It becomes easier for the student to talk in front of others. The student has taken a step toward developing self-confidence.

Listing strengths and weaknesses can help people improve their self-confidence.

[Chapter 10]

Setting Goals

People can set goals to improve their weaknesses. A goal is an objective people try to accomplish. People build self-confidence when they try to reach goals. They build more self-confidence when they reach their goals.

It is not easy to reach goals. It can take a long time to reach big goals. Some people set many small goals. These goals can be steps to reaching one big goal.

For example, a sales clerk's goal is to be a supervisor. The clerk lists the small goals needed to reach the big goal. The clerk needs to improve his computer skills. He needs to take special training courses. The clerk builds his self-confidence by reaching these goals and becoming a supervisor.

People who set goals want to improve. Successful people take the steps necessary to reach goals.

People build self-confidence when they reach goals.

Chapter 11

Showing Self-Confidence

People can show self-confidence in the ways they look and act. They can show they feel good about who they are. They can show they are proud of their abilities.

Self-confident people stand up straight. They make eye contact with others when they talk to them.

Some people show a lack of self-confidence. This can cause problems. For example, a store clerk looks down when talking to customers. The clerk's supervisor notices. The supervisor asks the clerk to look directly at customers. This shows customers the clerk wants to help them. It also shows that the clerk is confident about answering customers' questions.

People who show self-confidence can succeed. They show they are proud of their work.

People who show self-confidence can succeed.

Chapter 12

Self-Confidence and You

Self-confident people believe in their abilities. You can take steps to build your self-confidence. You can learn to believe in yourself.

Take pride in your appearance. You will feel more self-confident when you look your best. Work to have a positive outlook. Positive thinking helps build self-confidence.

Look for ways to improve your self-esteem. Think about your strengths. Set goals for improving your weaknesses. Take steps to reach your goals.

Remember that other people can help you build self-confidence. Accepting criticism can help you improve yourself. Accepting praise shows you have pride in yourself and in your work.

Building self-confidence takes time. You may need to take many steps. Taking these steps can be rewarding. With self-confidence, you will know you have the ability to succeed.

Other people can help you build self-confidence.

Words to Know

criticism (KRIT-uh-siz-uhm)—pointing out the strengths and weaknesses of others

customer (KUHSS-tuh-mur)—a person who buys goods and services

goal (GOHL)—an objective people try to accomplish

praise (PRAZE)—positive words about a person's actions or appearance

self-confidence (SELF KON-fuh-denss)—believing in one's abilities

self-esteem (SELF ess-TEEM)—a feeling of pride and respect for oneself

supervisor (SOO-pur-vye-zur)—a person who is in charge of workers

To Learn More

Johnson, Julie Tallard. *Celebrate You!: Building Your Self-Esteem*. Minneapolis: Lerner Publications Co., 1991.

Kramer, Patricia. *Discovering Self-Confidence*. New York: Rosen Publishing Group, 1991.

Schwartz, Stuart and Craig Conley. *Setting Career Goals*. Mankato, Minn.: Capstone High/Low Books, 1998.

Thomas, Alicia. *Self-Esteem*. New York: Rosen Publishing Group, 1991.

Useful Addresses

The Option Institute for Personal Growth
2080 South Undermountain Road
Sheffield, MA 01257

Success Dynamics Foundation
541 West 98th Street #183
Bloomington, MN 55420

Training Information Source, Inc.
1424 South Clayton Street, Suite 200
Denver, CO 80210

Internet Sites

America's Job Bank
http://www.ajb.dni.us/

Career Search
http://learningedge.sympatico.ca/
  careersearch/index.html

**Living on Your Own-Let's Calculate
  the Cost**
http://www.wnet.org/wnetschool/
  origlessons/lifecost/orgc.html

Self-Assessment
http://www.bsu.edu/careers/selfases.html

Index

action, 11, 17
appearance, 7, 17, 27

criticism, 19, 27

differences, 15

goals, 23, 27

mistakes, 19

positive outlook, 9, 27
praise, 17, 27
pride, 5, 27

respect, 5

self-esteem, 5, 13, 17, 27
steps, 5, 13, 21, 23, 27

worthwhile, 5, 13